CELEBRATING THE FAMILY NAME OF SPENCER

Celebrating the Family Name of Spencer

Walter the Educator

Silent King Books
a WhichHead Entertainment Imprint

Copyright © 2024 by Walter the Educator

All rights reserved. No part of this book may be reproduced in any manner whatsoever without written permission except in the case of brief quotations embodied in critical articles and reviews.

First Printing, 2024

Disclaimer

This book is a literary work; the story is not about specific persons, locations, situations, and/or circumstances unless mentioned in a historical context. Any resemblance to real persons, locations, situations, and/or circumstances is coincidental. This book is for entertainment and informational purposes only. The author and publisher offer this information without warranties expressed or implied. No matter the grounds, neither the author nor the publisher will be accountable for any losses, injuries, or other damages caused by the reader's use of this book. The use of this book acknowledges an understanding and acceptance of this disclaimer.

Celebrating the Family Name of Spencer is a memory book that belongs to the Celebrating Family Name Book Series by Walter the Educator. Collect them all and more books at WaltertheEducator.com

USE THE EXTRA SPACE TO DOCUMENT YOUR FAMILY MEMORIES THROUGHOUT THE YEARS

SPENCER

In fields of green and skies so clear,

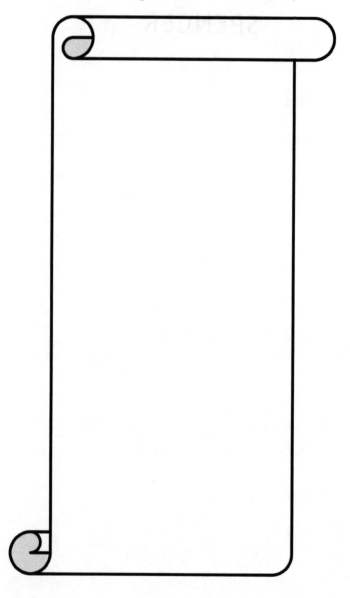

The name of Spencer rings sincere.

Through ages past and futures bright,

They walk in honor, bathed in light.

Strong roots extend from earth's embrace,

Deep in the ground, a storied place.

Their lineage vast, their spirits wide,

The Spencer name a source of pride.

Like oaks that stand in steadfast might,

They weather storms, they seek the right.

With wisdom passed from hand to hand,

Their legacy forever stands.

The Spencers stride with hearts so bold,

In warmth of summer, winter's cold.

They gather close in joys and tears,

In laughter rich that spans the years.

Their courage fierce, their kindness known,

In every heart, a garden sown.

Each branch that grows, each leaf unfurls,

In every boy and girl who twirls.

Through crafts and trades, through dreams and skill,

They shape the land with steadfast will.

From art to science, fields they sow,

In Spencer hands, great wonders grow.

A name that whispers strength and grace,

Its letters woven into space.

Like stars above, forever bright,

The Spencers rise, a beaconed light.

Though times may change and seasons shift,

The Spencers' hearts remain a gift.

A family bound in unity,

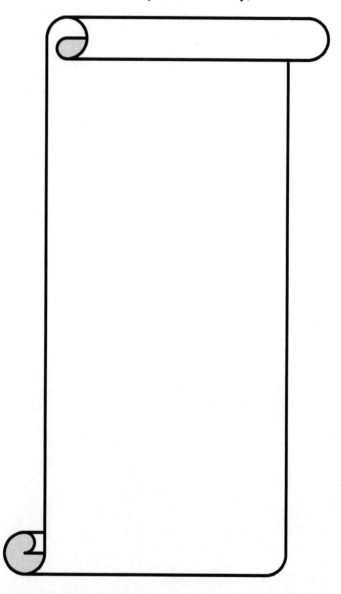

By love's eternal, lasting key.

They write their tales, they craft their song,

A melody both deep and strong.

With every step, they pave the way,

For brighter hopes and dawns of day.

So lift a toast to Spencers dear,

With voices loud, their name we cheer!

For in their bond, we find the truth,

Of love, of strength, and timeless youth.

ABOUT THE CREATOR

Walter the Educator is one of the pseudonyms for Walter Anderson. Formally educated in Chemistry, Business, and Education, he is an educator, an author, a diverse entrepreneur, and he is the son of a disabled war veteran. "Walter the Educator" shares his time between educating and creating. He holds interests and owns several creative projects that entertain, enlighten, enhance, and educate, hoping to inspire and motivate you. Follow, find new works, and stay up to date with Walter the Educator™

at WaltertheEducator.com